ANTOINE-HENRY LEMOINE

KINDER-ETÜDEN
EASY PROGRESSIVE STUDIES

für Klavier / for Piano

Opus 37

Herausgegeben von / Edited by
Adolf Ruthardt

ALLE RECHTE VORBEHALTEN · ALL RIGHTS RESERVED

EDITION PETERS
LEIPZIG · LONDON · NEW YORK

KINDER-ETÜDEN

Antoine-Henry Lemoine (1786-1854) op. 37
Herausgegeben von Adolf Ruthardt